5323

GREEN MOUNTAIN SCENERY.

No. 128

200 Stereoscopic and Card Views from all parts of Vermont.

PUBLISHED BY A. F. STYLES, BURLINGTON, Vt.

Catalogue sent free to any address.

125. Smuggler's Cave, Notch, Stowe, Vt.

Ed Roberson

kingfisher

for Kenny

Glimpse something drop   like fruit from a branch
of trees along the river   then fall back
up to its perch —   you've caught the kingfisher
burst from its dive,   back   into position
over the water,   nearly invisible reign;
Or just as explosively,   a stillness
pop out of the background   a blue —   heron.

Watching brings them   into being but for
their own coalescence   out of nothing
to do with us   any more than us with
them.   Interdependence   a scribbling
outside the lines   of what   we know to draw.
The sharpened quill   only closer draws itself
a feather   shaft to branch to barb and hook,

but never finally   fine enough to
nothing   between the wing and thin air
edges are   not the limit we thought.
Name outside itself,   of the subject hid
in itself   into its own pattern with   the ground,
the living eye must translate: diamond back
the stripe the spotted light   shadow into sight

back from nested camouflage   in the whole
of indeterminacy   back into flight
inside the lines   of time to stay itself
alive.   Where to step.   An underground

railroad guide's read.   tree or face.
Take Smuggler's Notch   the last leg to Canada.
You   can see down the climb for a day who's behind you   and
        there are caves   to fade into or appear
        out of   free

Kingfisher

Kingfisher
Matthew Goulish

for Lewis Washington

limnē

attention

Our words, our poems, begin by accident. This one begins with an accidental sighting *along the river.* When I say accident I mean interruption, and the redirection that follows, of what had been attention. Whatever had been subject of *that* attention lies now beyond the scope of the poem, of no consequence, forgotten in the void of the poem's outside. Now *this* attention takes hold if we allow it. How do they differ, these two attentions? One leads and one follows. The one that leads, we choose. The one that follows chooses us. The one that follows activates us beyond expectation. A glimmer, even a distraction, already past before it became present to us, how *do* we attend to it, this turning within a moment? The conflict between attention and distraction reveal's apprehension's dual polarity. The redirect between the two we now call to "pay attention with justice, the curiosity, and the evenhanded *just* curiosity." This second attention, that follows what we never sought, it will take us where we must go, if we have prepared properly to recognize it as guide. "Because, like the poem says, you have to be in a position to jump."

glimpse

To turn oneself around. To suggest that poetry does not begin with one's words at all, but with "being accosted" by that which one was not seeking. *Glimpse* and it has caught you, that sense of irreality, of the film running in reverse. The peripheral drop that one had no intention of seeing dropped as an ordinary interruption to attention. Newton's apple in its fall speaks of Newton's universe.

For that sidelong moment we think we live there. *then fall back up / to its perch* – The revelation of the impossible experience uncovers the fact of the world in the act of exceeding our mind's model of it. Cavell, speaking after Emerson, says: "It is where you first encounter yourself. It is where the sense of irreality of your existence and the necessity for turning yourself around first presents itself. The sense of irreality in 'Experience' is specified as a loss of the direction in which reality is to be found, that it is not ahead." Reality no longer constitutes our goal, prefigured, toward which we directed ourselves. We find it to one side. We find it only when it follows and allows us, when it illuminates, when, in activating itself, it calls to us and we hear and recognize the call. In turning to that horizon, in reversing course, we encounter ourselves. When Cavell replies "It is where..." the *it* refers to "the cave," in response to the question: "How is it that the cave is the actual ordinary?" In time we will speak more of justice—actual ordinary justice—and of caves.

breach

Immediately in beginning we must decide on breaks and how to read them. We must decide what precisely they connote. What exactitude do they score? We know something of line breaks. Reading all or nearly any poetry requires us to read their familiar potentials and multiplications of meanings. But this poet breaks mid-line. He adds spacings, manages inserts that part words within lines, spread word clusters from one another. When he reads his poems aloud, these spaces stop him with a micro-pause, a semi-breath. We might ask what these internal spaces offset. They prevent crowding. In this sense they introduce spaciousness. Spaces act as spacers. They will open up the alert words, that we may see as well as hear them, bunched like grapes in their graduated groupings. All of this makes of the usual spaces between words something unusual, not a given measure. Here's a common but strange rule: white space decelerates reading. Silently or aloud, the slowness the same, the care of distance between two words makes a presence of that emptiness. It insists itself like a bump for slowing. Every speed bump on any residential street emerges with its intransigent body like a whale's back, like a suspended manatee breaching the water's surface. It floats so still as if a rock could float, but alive. The vessel of my reading bumps over this "traffic calming" device. Anticipating the crest, I decelerate. I think more slowly. I might say more spaciously: space on the page, space in the mind.

reception

We distinguish the kingfisher sighting from the kingfisher's drop and return. The *you've caught*, the accidental intercept of the *nearly invisible reign*, the mode and manner of that apprehension—these make the habits of our common misapprehension known to us. Our outmoded manner of grasping what we take for the world produces this type of confused vision as much as the physics of this bird's dive and flight, its negotiations of gravity and the currents of water and air. In this way these distinctions of awareness produce a reflection of that which we apprehend. We might as easily have missed it. This compounding of reality on itself defines a transcendental relation. *Just as explosively* we might find ourselves ambushed by a heron, separated from its blue, which appears to us first as a condensation of unexpected color before the shape announces itself and with it the name *heron*. The space and the dash between words in the poet's line translate as time in this instance, the moment between perception and recognition, between *blue* and *heron*. In these revelatory configurations of freshwater and feathers, we experience the transcendental cascade. We find ourselves shaken by perceptual transcendence of habitual limits, rippling outward from the startling event, prompting us to question everything our fallible thinking has convinced us that we know. The instant of wakefulness awakens us to the ordinary breach between ourselves and the water bird. Henry Thoreau put the unbridgeability of this separation to the test with his attempts to anticipate the loon's trajectories below Walden Pond. We recall the man, the bird, the boat, the water's surface, and the game of chase and hide.

brute neighbor

"While he was thinking one thing in his brain, I was endeavoring to divine his thought in mine. It was a pretty game, played on the smooth surface of the pond, a man against a loon. Suddenly your adversary's checker disappears beneath the board, and the problem is to place yours nearest to where his will appear again." The stalking resembles a children's game. The swimming bird so routinely outmaneuvers the boatman, that the latter must wonder about the game's one-sidedness. Perhaps the bird does not play at all, but only follows the dictates of an altogether alien logic. "...he uttered one of those prolonged howls, as if calling on the god of loons..." This poet does not take recourse to such human projects or projections. He speaks, he writes, from experience, from familiarity with the unpathed wilderness. In refusal he critiques the common abstraction, and redraws fundamental relations. *Watching brings them   into being but for / their own coalescence   out of nothing / to do with us   any more than us with / them.* What nature of watching, we must ask now, brings *into being*, spanning such an unbridgeable divide? The break doubles the arrival: *out of nothing* and *out of nothing to do with us.* Thoreau will speak of this form of watching too in the end, this attention that creates: "Only that day dawns to which we are awake. There is more day to dawn." Always more, not infinite but inexhaustible, the horizon that appears when we attend to it, that unfolds before us.

draw

Another childlike activity—with its phrasing: *outside the lines*—suggests that apprehending these creatures with any degree of honesty returns us inevitably to second childhood. We must contend with *the lines*, and that which lies *outside* of them: the unfamiliar, the unknown but not unknowable. Regarding this *outside* as an area, an unfamiliar part of the given picture within its bounded frame, the poem enacts a shift to abstraction, to mediation and resemblance, of these material accidents of the sensible world, as Thoreau's behavior on the surface abstracts the submerged, invisible loon. We would draw only that which we can only envision. We cannot draw from beyond the mind's scope, from *outside the lines   of what   we know to draw.* Our experience so routinely outpaces what we think of as our knowledge; how do we render one of those episodes of radical encounter? How do we speak from it? How do we bring it in, that scribbling? In the effort and *out of the background* a pattern will surface and become legible. Through its haze of complexity we did not previously recognize pattern. In the realization, less recognition than rewriting out of the ungrounding, learning takes hold of us again as it once did, in childhood lessons, slower now, no less full of wonder, with a different vocabulary that still echoes the first, an altogether more pronounced set of stakes, the call of now, the cries of history. Feather, a word, and like a word, becomes the dimensive increment that individuates *blue* into *heron*. In these ways we draw the coexistence on which we have come to depend. We draw what we did not know, but come to know through the drawing. In drawing we think with our hands. The poet calls what we would draw this way, out of scribbling, *interdependence*. The word evokes the facts of shared resources: air, water, light—the reality of inseparable bodies, deindividualized, regrouped into a network existence. In depending we come to know ourselves as one body within many, with kingfisher, with heron, with loon, and with the waterways in the orbit of which we all find ourselves, one body with even ourselves, across the span of years. "In the poem time can surrender its mortal march to wilder horizons..." Where do we find this "in" of the poem, this interior where time surrenders? Where does this inside find us? Do we call it "reading"? Does it resemble the drawing we would make if we could actualize something more than scribble? Those questions will come back to us. What does their existence as questions tell us now?

What do we carry from them? We have arrived at an age from which we comprehend that in the profound de-impoverishment of the fleet kingfisher's moment we witness our own rebirth.

forms follow

Resonance of shapes that repeat flatten the known world into form. *The sharpened quill   only closer draws itself / a feather   shaft to branch to barb and hook,* In this regress of sourceless echoes, the tool attracts what it renders in its own likeness. Forms I know and name multiply until a proliferating forest of similarities invades my concourse. I navigate my way according to this constant consonance, this sounding together, that I cannot see without the help of seeing apparatus. I remove my glasses and wipe them to approach complete transparency. While doing so I see the world revert to blur. I begin to write. My pen becomes my lens. The keyboard I touch with its fixed and scattered alphabet and the trackpad I tap guide my mind. Some writers dictate their every observation to programs in devices that hear and recognize their voice, record and transcribe their words. They could write this way while sitting on a rock in a river. I will not call it not writing. Absolutely not; I depend on them. Still we know that no amplifying technology draws us closer to brain and reality. Every medium only draws thought differently. In some technologies, both supple and awkward, it seems my emotions settle and dwell there with elusive satisfaction. This ginkgo tree appears as it does in relation to my particular pencil. I walk the paths that I have written through the world. In this way the unaccountable wilderness recedes until, undeniable, it reveals itself to me with something more vertiginous than contradiction: the unimaginable. The poets gather our uncertainties. I rely on them, my guides. They bundle mysteries as closely as they can and bring them *but never finally   fine enough to / nothing*

the nameable

This poem that spoke for a moment near the start with a teacher's voice—*you've caught the kingfisher*—or a guide's, and that will do so again at the end, rounding off the reader's lesson in looking and identification, now turns inward. From interiority, and before coming out of introspection, it will puzzle out a problem of existence and appearance. Where patterns exist so too the possibility of the invisible. The living eye must translate in order to name, to draw out a figure from its ground. Life depends on that drawing out. The fact of life forever will foreground itself. In movement and in standing out against the fallen leaves, the living terrapin makes its claim, makes its presence known, no longer hidden or hiding in the invisibility of its stillness, becoming nameable: *diamond back*. We could call this another transcendent oscillation, between the poles of hidden and seen. The subject capable of hiding within itself can also present and announce itself. The poem has reversed its own problem as well as its own style. Introspection looks inward to inspect the interior. From what must one turn away? This question—once-removed, secondary, indirect, vital—conceals itself until we avert our gaze from the world. The poem asks now: what of this life-sustaining retreat?

immerse

Søren Kierkegaard in *Fear and Trembling* proposed faith's paradox, that "inwardness is higher than outwardness." "For the ethical view of life, the task for the single individual is thus to divest himself of the detriment of inwardness and express it in what is outward. Every time the single individual shrinks from doing this, every time he wants to hold back or disappear once again into the detriment of inwardness, into feeling, mood, etc., he is sinning—he is immersed in spiritual trial. The paradox of faith is this: that there is an inwardness that is incommensurable with the outer, an inwardness which, note well, is not identical with the first inwardness, but is a new inwardness." The philosopher wrote these words under the pseudonym John of Silence, speaking as if from such a place of retreat, to remind us precisely how every inward turn constitutes a turn to the spiritual, its inwardness "new," or a movement in the direction of renewal, that transgresses the ethical life, but that invites the pendulum swing of time, that makes of ethics a process necessitating the inclusion of its opposing movement. Here we find it as instantiation of this poet's signature maneuver: "a voice already on its way to becoming another voice." We risk a universal turn, defining poetry this way, as the language of this silence, the speech that issues from the turning away. Another poet, Robert Creeley, may have said as much in his own keen-eyed way when he declared of poetry, "Being there is the one requirement." That is to say, as he went on to say, poetry, the place of it, when we retreat there, we know as "that place we are finally safe in."

recoil

shadow into sight // back from nested camouflage   in the whole / of indeterminacy   back into flight / inside the lines   of time to stay itself / alive.   Where to step. When the return to movement returns us to the world, we find it and ourselves changed. The terrain brings to bear its measure of threat, and we have new knowledge and strategy for mapping its dangers and our place, our survival, and our movement among them. We can spot them coming if we keep watch behind, perhaps we even move forward while looking backward, considering where to put down a foot, and knowing ourselves when and how to disappear. *there are caves   to fade into or appear / out of   free* Anne Dufourmantelle wrote, "…a moment of conversion. Is it this gesture of the prisoner in Plato's myth of the Cave, his turning toward the true light?" Akiko Busch stated, "Our presence has to do not only with how we reveal ourselves, but also how we conceal ourselves." To turn oneself around, in that cave in Vermont, to retreat into the hollow of the actual ordinary, reconfigures the direction in which we find reality. It doubles the mind. In this cave we come to know the difference between the world and the world's image. We will know both ourselves and our resemblances. Our apprenticeship to the kingfisher constitutes nothing less than escape in place. We know no other definition of freedom than this—*to fade into or appear / out of*— freedom encoded in the potentiality of this humblest of words: *or.*

reading back / lake word

What has unified this poem's transit if not the waterway? Backgrounded, certainly, but omnipresent to the branching tributaries, the nested ideas issuing each with its own pace and carriage out of the previous. Living presence, quiet life source, the river runs. Its surface appears still, but in its depths it always flows with a movement of its own. "The moving waters at their priestlike task" of continuously becoming a vessel for common transport, set the pace and time signature. *from a branch / of trees along the river* and then *back into position / over the water* In the end, *the last leg to Canada* with its implicit Lake Champlain, the first pin on the map at the poem's last arrival. "—and there was a long period when you were working as a limnologist doing science related to waterways—" So a poet asked the poet. In doing so she invoked the core of the word, the formulation, at the heart of the poem: limnology, the study of the biological, chemical, and physical properties of lakes and other fresh-water bodies; a precious term that combines two roots, unlikely and now for us inseparable: *logos*, word, and *limnē*, lake. She asked him in a public conversation, "You've spent some portion of your career—I mean there was the period when you were working at the aquarium—and there was a long period when you were working as a limnologist doing science related to waterways—did you feel that the kind of quest for knowledge or quest for information or even quest for data that motivates so much of science in the history of, like, since the enlightenment, is some kind of choke hold, or is it better than that?" He replied: "A lot of times people just won't touch stuff. I think of myself as not letting go."

doubles

Take Smuggler's Notch   the last leg to Canada. Lines
ripe with double meanings turn the poem to its end.
The *Take* of consider, as if to say, "Consider now the case
study of Smuggler's Notch, on this particular route."
And as *An underground / railroad guide's read.* has set
the stage for this line's landing, the *Take* also sounds
as direction, speaking back through the generations to
those escaping, seeking the freedom partitioned by the
national borders inscribed on the map thus on the land,
the liberation meridian: "On this night, *take* the turning
that lands you at Smuggler's Notch." *An underground /
railroad guide* appears as both "a person familiar with
the area...taking a person or persons through the notch
to the other side" in that past historical moment, and a
guide book in our present; the possessive *read* both the
human guide's read of the signs in the terrain and the
read that we give to the published guide a century and a
half later. We read all according to this doubled image,
the polysemous hinge that grants us a dual place in the
folded time of the end of this poem. When we arrive at
the location of this landmark with its eponymous history
of smuggling goods north over the border, we find
ourselves both the smugglers and the smuggled. That
is to say, "we" smuggle "ourselves" when we identify
with those taking the route of the underground railroad
to freedom. *You can see down the climb for days who's
behind you* The direct address of the *You* doubles and
triples us. *You* as "one," as any one who travels and must
keep watch warily behind. *You* as "you," the addressee,
a traveller on the route, always already multiple, as the
escaping figures in history. And *You* as we travelers who

14

recreate their journey according to the *guide's read*, then again we readers guided in this journey by the poem, the journey of, and through, the poem, in the transit of reading, to arrive at all the meanings present, revealing themselves as they funnel into a final word *free*.

invisibilities

It is not only race that makes its presence known, for those who can recognize it, in the invocation of the underground railroad, but also the originary sin of the United States, built in savage inequality, forced labor, fallacies of superiority and ownership. All of this remains the necessary background to the movement away from it in the communal transport to freedom; and in the lines of flight, the unrecorded strategies, labors, and mappings of abolitionists. The meaning of the imperative to keep watch on retrospective views also multiplies—to look out for any in pursuit, and to keep an eye on one's own past. *and / there are caves   to fade into or appear / out of* We have said already that in the cave, "It is here that you first encounter yourself," but now we know this cave as only a stop on *the last leg* the middle space between the past's captivity and the future's freedom, the stoppage of the cave, with its micro-reversal, a temporary perch within a life in motion. Benjamin Voight refers to one characteristic that defines this poet's work and makes it challenging, as "sudden inversions of argument." We might trace the trope of visibility to one memorable source in the first line of Ellison's novel: "I am an invisible man." We understand this concept less as argument than as undeniable and insistent nexus: a circulation of image that appears and vanishes in equal measure—the image that disappears, the image of disappearance—and for Ellison's narrator, the alienation of going unseen: unseen as an individual because seen only as the representative of a group; literally unseen as overlooked and of no consequence, disposable; and finally invisible because of hiding oneself away from view, in an underground cavern or in the disguised identity of another. But now this poet, once a limnologist, works his inversion. Time in the wild has taught him the power of disappearance; in this case inversion not at all sudden, but preconditional. *tree or face.* It constitutes a form of backtracking, of thought in reverse, beyond its presumed originary point, a reversal that any consideration of the non-human proposes again and again. Kingfisher, heron, loon, terrapin, all testify to the force of the hidden. Reversal actualizes inversion. In the conspicuous journey from captivity to freedom, one must understand how and when to embrace stillness and invisibility.

returns

The poem arrives at its end, a departure. Moving through it, the *You*, the we, return *back into flight / inside the lines.* "There are, though, more complex matters involved in what I've said. Who is the we I mean?" In the spectralism of we, the prismatic effect of that troubled wedge-shaped word, lies its angular operation to distribute the many out of one, to reveal and embrace the range of proximities to restless apparitions from a past already multiple, always moving. We the reader, all of us, however distant our starting points, the we that this poet and this poem trusts in, risks and invites, returns to flight, a fast word connoting both escape and taking to air. It returns us to inside the lines, which might mean filling in with color the shapes and fields bounded by, defined by, precisely drawn outlines, as a child does who plays at appearances; while also meaning *inside the lines* of the poem, the written lines that designate the place of their own creation. Where is that interior twilight? The poem becomes the cave *to fade into or appear / out of* We readers return to this sheltered space, and in the end return to the world released by the final word *free. the living eye must translate*: must make of itself the living I. In this visibility and disappearance, the I has come to know two modalities of existence and two textures of time; it, or as we must now say, we, staying alive, and becoming and remaining ourselves *back into flight / inside the lines of time to stay itself / alive* to turn in the end, irreversibly changed, to that state which the poem may fairly call *free*, inaugurated by the geography of freedom, and into which we humans find ourselves ushered by the returning strangeness of the kingfisher.

Correspondence

More than one friend has named as favorite the kingfisher. When regarding birds, what exactly does favoritism mean? I wonder in particular about such attachment for non-birders, for those of us who devote our lives to this or that discipline that considers birds if at all only peripherally, but who nevertheless stop and notice. Two talked to me specifically about this bird's head. Jack, an architect, texted me that he "used to see them along the Boardman River near Traverse City" in northern Michigan. "The size of its head in relation to its length is both odd and captivating." I remember riding in a car with Iris, a horse trainer, driving near Harvard, Illinois where, she said, she would occasionally spot one near that area's lakes. She described how the bird projected its upper parts forward in flight, giving it the appearance of awkward vulnerability. "I'm worried about your head." She spoke as if addressing the kingfisher. "Isn't that dangerous? Can't you pull it in?"

I have a large volume to which I turn frequently, and not only in writing this: the *Smithsonian Handbooks Birds of North America Western Region* by Fred J. Alsop III. I have just now for the first time taken a moment to review all of the nine birds that it pictures on its cover, each with its identifying name in small text immediately below the image: Acorn Woodpecker, Lesser Goldfinch, Allen's Hummingbird, Red Phalarope, Sharp-shinned Hawk (the large centerpiece), American Woodcock, Bobolink, Verdin, and Belted Kingfisher. What would we call this striking collection if not an assembly of favorites? These cover images depict seven birds perching, one (Red Phalarope, noted in the book as "pelagic in winter") swan-like on water's surface, and one in dramatic flight: the kingfisher, wings extended back, head thrust forward.

This encyclopedic handbook brings birds to my attention. It tells me that they exist, "out there," and shares its portraiture of appearance, behavior, and migratory patterns, in clinical detail, with maps and diagrams. Ed Roberson's poem does something altogether different. For me it stands in for a sighting. Maybe in this way it operates as a secular prayer, to grant a wish for such an encounter. I would like to see for myself this creature's wrongness, the off-balance build that enchants not only my friends but apparently nearly everyone. We seem to hold a special place in our hearts, we who care about such things, for asymmetries: the fiddler crab with one outsized claw, the top-heavy pelican. Do we identify with them, these perfect imperfections? Do we aspire to them? Maybe this captivation, this casual hold they have over us, and this concern, reflects back to us a soul, our own, inhering in a spirit or guardian creature. It will appear at our crucifixion. If only we were to know it. As the testimonies of my two noted friends make clear, we must see for ourselves in order not only to believe but also to adopt, to project these creatures inward as companions. In childhood fishing trips overnight to Northern Michigan for sunfish and even up into Canada for walleye pike, I heard the loon over the lake. The high extended pitch and its fall into decrescendo seemed a voice cast out across the placid expanse. The sounds became one with morning mist dissipating at dawn. Amazingly to me, the only image I had for the unseen bird had been impressed onto a Canadian coin like a totem, authenticating what I had experienced as its mysterious importance. I made a point of keeping one in my pocket and taking it out to look at it, or simply touching it, when I heard the call, transmission from the "code figure of birds" as Roberson wrote in another poem:

come morning   thin air   augury's loon
singing its insides out out of sight: a dew.

Now I wonder about those like the kingfisher whose presence I have never experienced. The handbook describes its call as "Bold raspy rattle sounds like a heavy fishing reel." Philosopher Charles Hartshorne, better known for his process theology, wrote one book that he described as "An Interpretation and World Survey of Bird Song." In the chapter on "The Less Well-Equipped Singers," he states, "The kingfisher group consists almost entirely of visually distinctive, poorly concealed birds, many of them fairly large. They live in 'open forests.' They are mostly without music."

I treasure the strange creature that I have come to know from this portrait, cobbled from any available secondhand description, and from the encyclopedic statistics, like the star charts of Walt Whitman's *Learn'd Astronomer*—"the proofs, the figures, ranged in columns before me, the charts and diagrams, to add, divide, and measure them." But unlike Whitman, I cannot walk out to apprehend, as simply and reliably as gazing up at the night sky in 1867, the truant kingfisher, as if the bird has a responsibility to show up for me. Until I have a sighting of my own, the kingfisher occupies a hallowed place, consecrated like the objective of a quest, but not an "object," a sentient creature with its own necessities that have nothing to do with me. I ask then, will the kingfisher show itself to me, or anyway show itself in my presence, at a moment when I am able to pay the right kind of attention? Until that occasion, which may never come, stuck more or less as I am for an unknown duration here in this pocket of Chicago, I thought this poem would substitute. But it has only compounded the strangeness. It presents the act of fishing, down and back again, like a further impossibilization of this bird, this king of the material accident. At this point in my life, with no other expectation, I turn to this poet. He has crafted an intimate knowledge of the bird and an intricate language for the intimacy. I look out and listen in. I trace it as best I can. This one came to me as so many seem to that refuse to leave, by a circuitous coincident path.

§

The Poetry Foundation invited us (the performance group *Every house has a door*, Lin Hixson director, myself dramaturg) to present an early version of our performance *The Three Matadores*, a staging of a play within a poem by Jay Wright. Ed Roberson attended that performance, and afterward the Events Coordinator from the Foundation who had invited us introduced me to him. I recognized the name, but at that time knew little of the poetry. I recalled the publication of *City Eclogue* in the series co-edited by Lyn Hejinian, a West Coast poet who had long been an important figure for me and for so many. Ed spoke to me quietly and generously about our performance, and about Jay's writing that he believed clearly announced itself, through all of the multi- and inter-cultural allusions, maybe because of them, as distinctly American. The conversation stayed with me, as did the memory of the voice and the presence. Soon my reading turned in his direction. How differently we read the words when we hear in our mind the voice of the writer. I began with *To See the Earth Before the End of the World*, published in 2010. That prompted me to go back to the beginning, to begin reading the earliest published works and to continue through as many books as I could find. The poet's history as not only a naturalist but also as a practicing scientist, with all the rigor and authority the term implies, made itself known.

> I lived in that cabin by the lake on the job
> at the research station, taking into the bog
> of dew-mirrored water lilies, the mist-damp boat
> to gather water samples daily after dawn.

I resisted the hall of mirrors of literary reference through which one may learn to study contemporary poetry, reading lines such as *the mist damp boat / to gather water samples* as my invitation to such resistance, considering *Kingfisher* less (that is, not at all) through the lens of Charles Olson (*The Kingfishers*), and more by way of the bird among actual birds, accepting the chance to contemplate what it provokes, taken as a form of homecoming. This is not to say this poet does not know his literary history or writes as a total outsider. He will speak of the importance of George Oppen, *Of Being Numerous* in particular. Rather I believed that any allusions embedded in his work operate in a minor key, as secondary textures from a poet who announces his priorities clearly, whose poems trace their complex courses transparently. They challenge us not to decode them but to follow where they lead, to keep pace with the complexity of their unfolding logic.

At the time we, that is *Every house*, had commenced work on a series of performances following the fourteen movements of *Carnival of the Animals*, the 1886 musical suite for children by Camille Saint-Saëns. When the pandemic intervened, we transformed and reduced our performance *Aquarium* into a short film, produced with the three performers safely spaced from one another in the cold open air of fall 2020. We needed something, some words, to provide context for this strange, silent, imaginary sea world in which eccentrically costumed performers, in garments designed and constructed by Finnish artist Essi Kausalainen, appear as an electric ray, a strand of eyelash seaweed, and a quivering branch of coral/limestone before the camera's indifferent unedited sweep that records the contrasting time signatures of their choreography. The Poetry Foundation forwarded our inquiry to Ed Roberson. In writing it, I had recounted our brief meeting and conversation after our performance of Jay Wright's *Matadores* play, before requesting permission to extract 14 lines for our film.

> The sea
>   has always had
> its peace
>   through shell to say
>
> how much
>   each wave ending
> a zero more
>   it can't sit still

The hearth's conch
   its breath   curling
an echo of the steam
   engine boogie drumming

   of train track blues
is really attuned   of the heart.

We would open our film with these words appearing on the screen, allowing even the slow reader ample time, and then bring them back at the end in the form of lyrics for a song, composed and performed by Madeleine Aguilar. I soon received an email reply.

Sat, Oct 10, 2020, 5:41 PM

Dear Matthew,

Alex Benjamin at the Poetry Foundation kindly forwarded me your letter. Thank you very much for your interest in my work and for wanting to make it a part of your own. You have my permission to use those 14 lines of mine in your Aquarium performance project. Could you let me know which poem it is that you'll be taking the excerpt from?

You might be interested to know that one of my upcoming books will contain a section called "Twenty Aquarium Works," which are poems written about my time as a diver/tankman at the Pittsburgh Aquazoo in the 1960s. If you're interested in reading it at some point, I'd be happy

25

to send that sequence to you.

I've copied my assistant, Andrew Peart, on this email. He can help with any details moving forward.

Yrs,
EdR

Nion Editions published *Aquarium Works* in 2022 in a volume that included an appendix with prose descriptions by the author of *Ten of the Fauna Mentioned (in order of appearance)*. Back in 2020, I was of course overjoyed to receive this reply, since it allowed our film project to go forward as intended. The lines appear in the poem *When Change* in the 1999 book *Atmosphere Conditions*. Alongside my joy, or within it like a stowaway, nestled my captivation by two incidental words: "tankman" and "Aquazoo." These artifacts of a lexicon, specialized in usage but transparent in meaning, resonated along with the idea of *the 1960s*. The decade had so defined me, born as I was in January of 1960, that it had become for me, and I think for many, a very durable idea. Somehow these two new words belonged in that idea. They returned in the podcast conversation that the Poetry Foundation produced between Ed Roberson and his interlocutor of choice, Lyn Hejinian. I will come to that conversation in time. I had turned to it soon after receiving the invitation from Sam Ladkin to write what would become the two-part essay, if I may call it an essay, if I may call it two-part, that you are now reading. Maybe two essays describes it better, or three. They proceeded in parallel in their creation and thought, although this one always intended to follow after the other. They each supply what the other cannot. Such is the nature of discourse, the aporia between performance and conversation, or something like that. The invitation sounded the wake-up call to both.

Tues, Jul 6, 2021, 7:47 AM

Dear Matthew,

I'm writing to invite you to contribute to a new series of long essays (or whatever other genre of critical prose might best describe whatever work you might produce), to be published by a new imprint called Both Are Worse: Poetry and Poetics, run by a group of people working at the University of Sussex. We hope to commission around 8 or so essays for the first batch of the series. We'd be delighted if you would write one of them.

We expect the project to take shape and find its directions once it gets underway, but as a rough guide to a starting position, the idea is to assemble works of critical prose of between 15,000 and 30,000 words that make an engaging comment on the state of poetry and/or poetics now, stretch some horizons, push out beyond an impasse, heap up obstructions, or make life more difficult or liveable in any way that seems compelling, vital or beautiful. Studies of single authors, histories of communities or forms, manifestos, treatises on metre, philosophies of phonation, provocations of every stripe and blotch, dream diaries, long jokes, spreadsheets or inscrutable swirls of one-dimensional Venn diagrams would all be great. Anything that works.

Do let us know if you have any questions or if there is anything more we could tell you.

Best wishes,

Sam Ladkin

on behalf of the editors.

I deeply appreciated how Sam's invitation gave a wide berth to the languages of art history and literary theory, two modes I had come to regard as less entertaining forms of zombie drag. The pandemic world had annihilated my appetite for academic discourses which seemed to me to presume a common nostalgia that I did not share for quote unquote normal times. A worldwide decimating virus had forced on humanity certain necessary transformations that we had not had the foresight or will to undertake on our own, and gradations of denial ranged from the conspiratorial extreme to more mundane failures of imagination. Two practices, I believed, had kept pace with the rapidity of pandemic demands, had in fact been prepared and even anticipated the need: biochemistry and poetry. Katalin Karikó's persistent work on the poetically named Messenger RNA proteins that communicated their directives to cell behavior had laid the groundwork for humanity's current and perhaps undeserved reprieve from extinction, while the practices of poets had given us the language for understanding the spiral in which we, the embattled, embittered, explosive, innocent, ridiculous, myriad worldwide community of the human, found ourselves. Sam's invitation managed itself with care and humor, its life force apparent and itself a rejoinder to the grimness of the time of its arrival. I turned to the poem that, for all its gentleness of voice, had grounded me the most unfailingly, even ferociously, reflecting back the same life force. If I needed this so badly, experience had taught me, others must need it as well. As if accepting a fantasy assignment, I resolved to write as best I could the tributaries leading into, and the superpositional concentricities emanating out from, *Kingfisher*.

My time to begin writing coincided with a fall semester in which my teaching duties involved advising, remotely over a video-conferencing platform, graduate writing students on their work. One such "student," also a teacher at another institution and a father of two, scraped together enough time to complete a degree. I distinctly remember the oddly angled shelves stacked with folded garments behind his looming face and disheveled hair during the 55-minute meeting in which, in order to muster the necessary concentration, he sequestered himself in a closet. With so little time to write, he often missed deadlines and spoke instead about the work of other writers, passages or even sentences that he admired and taught in his classes. In one such conversation he brought up Renee Gladman's 2016 book *Calamities*, in particular the day in which the author describes a complex lecture on poetry that she attempts to deliver to a classroom full of unreceptive students. I had also taught excerpts from this work, a sort of prose daybook every section of which begins with the same four words: *I began the day...* Passages then diverge, each in its own direction, and the collection builds itself in echoes and accumulations of varying length and tone. In my class I had concentrated on the first five days, which I had read closely and repeatedly, so had forgotten about the day of the lecture further into the volume. I returned to it now after our conversation, and to my astonishment rediscovered the subject of her lecture.

I began the day looking up at the whiteboard, wondering how I would do the thing that I needed to do. My students were waiting. Robert Frost was their contemporary picture of poetry. I didn't think this would help them with Ed Roberson. I was going to try to draw a grid of light, as if one were looking down upon it, a grid that extended across an opaque surface, then draw, a good distance below that, a container, inside which were symbols. From the lower container, I wanted to draw lines that reached the opaque surface then became the actual lines of the grid. I would call those lines emanations. Without being essentialist, or perhaps being only momentarily so, I wanted to say, Often when reading poetry, it's the grid you're experiencing, and the grid is not the same things as that subterranean container, where some meaning might lie, the actual story of the poem, rather it's the shape of the emanations refracted through language and feeling (though many contemporary poems have no feeling) that you're reading. I didn't know how to draw the effect of looking down on something, so I asked for a volunteer. Someone tall offered, and as I was looking up at his attempt to look down, I realized that there was a flaw to my thinking. The place from which the emanations arose was not intact, it was not a container wherein lay meaning. It was a grid itself but of what I could not explain within the allotted time. I had to let the class go: it was 3:51, one minute into their "free" time. I couldn't find my words; they remained sitting there. How could I send them off to read Roberson's book without having explained poetry to them. "There is a grid above and a grid below," I said slowly, trying not to uplift my voice into a question. Perhaps to read poetry was to read through a sieve. I wanted to incorporate the idea of a matrix. "Poetry comes out of nothing," I said, opening something I would never be able to close. 3:52. "Read the nothing," I shouted after them as they walked out the door.

I think about teaching's urgency. I mean the necessity, so often one-sided, that pressurizes the teacher's every utterance, the imperative to impart knowledge, or discover knowledge together, intertwined tasks that verge on the impossible, since no available language exists for the most pressing ideas and their most effective mode of communion. One must perform a necessary reinscription of the world. This teacher participates in the speculative inquiry while guiding it, orchestrating the encounter and setting its frame, speaking less as an authority on the subject than as a more experienced traveler through the terrain. The venture turns comical perhaps if students do not share in the *conatus*, the impulse and the striving, or recognize, for whatever reason, the teacher as the desired form of authority. The teacher's acceptance of herself as a student of the subject guides the lesson, and this in itself disconcerts a student who suspects in it a pedagogical displacement. She, the teacher, signals from that threshold in which pattern emerges out of chaos, and not everyone will welcome or even grasp the fearlessness and honesty of that approach. But what do people think teaching is, after all? I often ask myself this question when I receive a syllabus guide for the remote classroom that bludgeons me with terms like "content delivery," as if the conceptual administration of education has been infected by a thought virus from distribution services. Consider the diagram. Philosopher Wahida Khandker has written that "drawing and diagram-making can serve as a means of thinking differently about what it means to be a living organism." Her interest in the diagram concerns "principally, its activity or enactment, and secondarily, its status or use as a representational form." How can the imagination represent the complexity of the act of reading a poem, or poetry in general, and the process by which understanding emerges in the act of reading, in lines and forms flattened to two dimensions? And why do so? "Drawing is," writes Khandker, "part of our enactment of time. We are not 'in' time, in the manner that objects occupy parts of space. We *are* time, unfolding at different speeds. Time, if any 'thing,' is a heterogeneous multiplicity of speeds and slownesses (as Deleuze phrases it). Thus, when one draws, one acts and thinks temporally." In Gladman's instance we witness the emergent character of her diagram, we watch as it transforms, the transformation a form of correction in the moment of its enactment, proving its power to guide thinking's accuracy, to materialize the act of thought in time.

And what about Robert Frost? This maligned poet stands in for the dissonance between poetry's necessity and its image of itself. While his name has become synonymous with an outmoded and overexposed poetics, his actual poetry may offer a perfectly good starting place for understanding Ed Roberson. I take down my copy of *A Further Range* and turn to *The White-Tailed Hornet*. But why argue the point? The Robert Frost of *The White-Tailed Hornet* almost never coincides with the one people have in mind when they invoke the name, and the one whom the described students must recognize. In any case, this teacher's adventures in the understanding of poetry, and specifically of Roberson, the rare and valuable poetics of her teaching, make their own unflinching demands on the image and act of thought as poetry's precondition. She distinguishes three operative forces—container, grid, and emanation—and binds them in successive levels through a diagram that, as described, predicts her *Plans for Sentences* (2022) with its extended proof of the indelible relation between writing and drawing. I had been blessed, the year before the pandemic, with an opportunity bestowed on me by chance, to hear Renee Gladman read from her work. She had in fact read from *Calamities*. I introduced myself and spoke with her after the event. In those moments I felt we had made a connection lasting enough to recollect without too much effort. Inspired, or goaded, by Sam Ladkin's correspondence, I composed an email. It included this paragraph.

I am starting a hopefully long essay on the poem *Kingfisher* by Ed Roberson from his 2021 book *Asked What Has Changed*. I have read and reread the day in *Calamities* (pages 34 & 35) that you devote to recreating a diagram guide for reading his poetry, distinct from the poetry of Robert Frost, yet also in some ways abstractable to all poetry. But now, in re-reading these two pages, I wonder whether in fact your image, interrupted by the end of class, applies to all of Ed

Roberson's poetry, or only to the book you had at that time assigned to the class. May I ask which book that was, if you recall? I am operating on the assumption that the episodes in *Calamities* actually happened, which I believe you indicated, in our conversation after your reading, they had. If you feel the inclination and have the time to engage with this inquiry, I of course welcome any more thoughts you might have, or lesson plans, or actual diagrams, or marginalia, or whatever you would like to share regarding ER's poetry. If you choose not to engage or cannot, I certainly understand. In any event those passages of *Calamities* that circulate in the weave of pedagogy, poetry, and essay, continue to guide my thinking and writing.

Five days later, on a Sunday, I received this reply.

Sun, Sep 5, 2021 9:39 AM

Dear Matthew,

It's lovely to hear from you. Yes, I remember fondly meeting you in Chicago and our conversation over your book. It's exciting to hear about the essay you're writing on Roberson's poem *Kingfisher*. Will you please let me know when it's published? It's a stunning piece; I spent a lot of yesterday with it. As for the Calamity, someone just asked me about that in an interview/conversation. How funny. This was a translator and she was trying to convey how that image of the grids resembled her thinking about her translation practice. In any case, the book in question was *To See the Earth Before the End of the World*, published in 2010 I think. The class in which I taught the book was 10 years ago so I don't remember that much about it any more. I mean, I don't remember which parts were real and which were embellished for the book. In *Calamities*, I always started in/with some aspect of a real event in my life and then let the "facts" follow whatever the energy or thinking of the line/paragraph needed. That class did lead me to asking over the years, "Where is the poem exactly"? Because it was clear that it was not on the page but also not exactly in me, the reader, either. I think that's why the two grids formed, because of the immediate elsewhere language creates when it's read. So, that's that. I hope this is useful. And thanks for asking.

All my best,
Renee

I have thought, although not in this way precisely, of what RG refers to as the immediate elsewhere, the sense that the poem transports the entranced reader to a specifically placed environment, a pin on a map of a world that resembles our own with certain amplifications. I say "not in this way precisely" because I had not thought about the poem per se existing in that place as much as the affect of the poem. Now concerning this concept—*the immediate elsewhere language creates when it's read*—consider the question in the particular context of *Kingfisher*. The poem's immense value may inhere in the access it grants to this elsewhere. That thought having occurred to me transported my thinking back to Aquazoo—the word, not the place. The place I could only try to imagine. The word and its elsewhere I now felt had become a part of me. It took me back to the October 2020 conversation interview between Ed Roberson and Lyn Hejinian, somewhat to my ear oddly referred to as a podcast by The Poetry Foundation. I mean, is every recorded interview a "podcast" now? What and where is the "pod" exactly? Does that half of the word refer to the iPod, the device which no longer exists upon which these types of conversations first found distribution? And regarding the "cast," I remember in my middle school science teacher's lessons on radio the distinction between broadcast and narrowcast. In those instances the casting, the "sowing by scattering" as a farmer with seeds, in fact described the event of waves emanating and publicly receivable by any in the area, broadly or narrowly, with the appropriate technology. The private act of loading a recorded conversation, once you purchase it, directly into your device, supplants and inverts the idea of public soundspace. It perversely even cannibalizes its verb "to cast," because nothing has been cast at all. In fact the term falsifies itself. The fact of direct communication only into a pod negates the possibility of casting, unless we invoke the pod as itself a container of seeds, or even the pod that we know as a small herd or school of marine mammals, especially whales. Thus we return to Aquazoo. An exchange commences at the 10:50 point, with Hejinian's assessment of Roberson's intent.

LH: Heraclitus, part of his philosophy, pivots around the question of justice, and justice is where there's perfect balance. And that change—like the sun goes to the solstice, and then to the other solstice, and then back again—if it didn't do that, if it went just to one solstice, it would be cheating the other one. And the middle place is the place of justice. The word is *dikai.* There is just thematically, as you're writing about what's happening to the climate, and also what's happening to people of the non white hegemonic power structure, especially Black and brown people, so race and environment, which are really interwoven in your poems, it seems like the quest is for justice, or harmony, or balance, and that every poem is trying to assert the presence of balance and justice and harmony. Is that an accurate description?

ER: That's exactly right.

These ideas return at about 19:45 and continue through the dialogue that I transcribed as best I could.

LH: You've spent some portion of your career—I mean there was the period when you were working at the aquarium—and there was a long period when you were working as a limnologist doing science related to waterways—did you feel that the kind of quest for knowledge or quest for information or even quest for data that motivates so much of science in the history of, like, since the enlightenment, is some kind of choke hold or is it better than that?

ER: You know a lot of times people just won't touch stuff. I'm saying choke hold because I think of myself as not letting go. But really I think it's that willingness to pick up a rock or pick up anything and look at it, rather than just look at it and walk by, as though it isn't doing anything. [...]

LH: There's a couple of places that reminded me a little bit of George Oppen, and his almost reverence for just what is, and his quest to write a poetry that simply said "it is." And I think that something like that, or like *Choke*, all of these poems in this particular group of poems of yours are [...] manifestations of picking things up by wording them, to look at them, sniff them, see what kind of shadow they cast, put them down carefully again, a kind of elaborate perceiving process.

ER: That's right. That's what I'm trying to do. I know of George Oppen—I'm kind of shocked, you see—I like that work and I'm happy you see that in my work.

LH: And he too was poet who was looking for balance, justice, and also always felt ambivalent, or often, like in the long poem *Of Being Numerous*.

ER: My favorite.

LH: Of course, it's a masterpiece. But he's like, the world is way too complicated, to come to a final position, which I think has so much integrity, to say I don't have the answer, but here's what I've seen. And curiously, that poem ends with the word "curious." I just remembered that. And you and I, when we first started talking today, we both said despite all of the terrible, catastrophic, possibilities that are facing us really soon, that we remain almost naively curious. Like, what *is* gonna happen, and then what, and then what?

ER: Because out of the curiosity, anybody might be able

to offer a portion of the answer. People who pay attention, and pay attention with justice—I'm glad you brought that up too—they'll be able to give a portion of what is a possible answer, and it won't be just for that particular person. It'll be for many people. And that's what you want. So I think the curiosity, and the evenhanded, *just* curiosity, is where we should be. I don't see myself being able to survive anywhere else. Cause like the poem says, you have to be in a position to jump.

§

On September 2nd, two days after I wrote to Renee Gladman, I cast out another line in the form of a letter on paper sent through the mail to Michelle Arnosky Sherburne, historian of abolition and the Underground Railroad in New Hampshire and Vermont. My essay, I thought, needed one more voice to fill in the background of the final turn in *Kingfisher* with its tenor of heightened vigilance. The materials that resulted from this inquiry, and from the historian's extraordinary generosity, in a correspondence with me that lasted two years, became so substantial that I will devote the next section of this essay entirely to them.

Before relinquishing the floor to Michelle Sherburne, I will offer my own conclusion, a simple one, to this essay, or this part of the larger essay. If the second, it remains provisional, which is perhaps best, for the restraint to which it subjects my voice. This conclusion, if I may call it that, makes of my function as writer a tentative one, which must have in this part by now become apparent.

Anyway, the conclusion is this. Reading a poem properly becomes out of necessity a collective endeavor. By reading I mean considering every receivable element, from the poet's initial act of composition, the devising or isolating of its immediate elsewhere, to the material inking of the words, settled on the common transport of their pages, sequenced between their covers, to the conceptual returns of every resonance, the meanings and branching interpretations, and all the impalpable tributes of context. By collective I mean, I must mean, community, however loosely defined and porous, of colleagues and strangers whom the poem brings together. The poem catalyzes friendship, then, if we let it. It becomes our communion. We have the poem, if even nothing else, in common.

§

Smuggler's Notch

Good morning Matthew,

Thank you for reaching out to me! I apologize for not responding sooner, it's been a bit hectic!

First, thank you for reading my book. It is a sampling of the history that is out there on the subject! I could have written a 300 page book if I could have found a publisher for it!!

That's why I travel around VT and NH lecturing to share more of what I have discovered!

I will look into your question about Smuggler's Notch and the reference in Ed Roberson's *Kingfisher* poem. I haven't had a chance to dig into it but I do have one piece of information that might be helpful.

No I don't have any research pertaining to Smuggler's Notch at the moment but when I looked at my Siebert map, I see there's something.

It's a start.

I am attaching Wilbur Siebert's VT/NH map of the locations of safehouses and also lines of travels (routes/trunk lines) that he researched. I use Siebert's work as a base point of research because he did extensive work on the subject. I reference him in my book.

Not only did Siebert write a number of books on the

43

Underground Railroad across the country (Northern states) his correspondence and notes are available at Ohio Historical Society online.

If you look at the attached map, Siebert had a line of travel for Freedom Seekers through Lamoille County on the western side of Vermont, near Burlington, St. Albans. The red lines are Siebert's. So I see it goes through Jeffersonville which is where Smuggler's Notch is located.

Let me take some time to review Siebert's files and look through mine to see if anything direct references.

And also I want to look into the *Kingfisher* poem as well. Interesting that he used a Vermont location and not something closer to home!

I ask for your patience and I will be back in touch shortly.

Once again, thank you for reaching out. I am happy to help!

Take care!
Michelle Sherburne

Fri, Oct 29, 5:07 AM

Good morning Matthew,

Hope you are doing well!

I have done some initial research about Ed Roberson's references to the Vermont Underground Railroad in *Kingfisher.*

Thank you for introducing his work and this poem to me. I have learned so much!

Not only of his style but of my own subject of the Underground Railroad.

In the 30 years of researching, "new" information surfaces and so my quest is never-ending! How great is that!

In the "dissertation" (I don't know what else to call it!) I do note that I had not researched Smugglers' Notch and its usage during the Underground Railroad era. That is not uncommon, if it didn't come across my research radar, and people didn't mention it to me, then I don't have anything on it, just as in other cases. But doing a search online, I did find references to it now.

A disclaimer of sorts for the PDF file I attached: In it I use the term "fugitive slave" which I am accustomed to doing and have done in my books. Very recently, in the past year or so, I have been made aware of people who find that offensive and want the term "enslaved" instead of "slave" or "freedom seeker" instead of "fugitive slave." When I give history presentations now, I try to be sensitive to the audience.

But as an historian, writer and newspaper person, I understand the term "fugitive slave" as what they actually were: one, they were slaves, owned by another person, i.e., property; two, they were fugitives because they were fleeing their owners and breaking the law (as were the Underground Railroad agents who aided them).

Also in the disclaiming mode, I use the term "Underground Railroad agent" and not necessarily "stops" or "safehouses" because I try to focus on the people who did the assisting! And "agent" best describes these people because it was a dedication and commitment to be "on call" when needed. Plus it falls in line with the acceptable railroad terminology that was used from the 1840s to 1860s.

So I hope I am not offending you. And you can use my essay and change those terms if you want. No problems there.

And yes if you want to use any or all of what I sent you.

I cropped Wilbur Siebert's map to the area around Smugglers' Notch so the references to Underground Railroad agents in surrounding towns is easier to follow. I don't have an exact date on the Siebert Vermont/New Hampshire map. But the Ohio Historical Society Manuscript Collections has the bulk of Siebert's work dating from 1892 to 1951.

I hope that you will find information I am providing to be of assistance in your work.

Again, I thank you for introducing the poem and Ed

Roberson's work to me. I have gleaned so much that
I will be able to use in future lectures and possibly in
future books.

Take care. All the best,
Michelle

I found Ed Roberson's bio and learned that he was born in Pittsburgh, PA, went to University of Pittsburgh and then completed his graduate work at... Goddard College... in East Montpelier, VT! That explains why a Pennsylvania native who lives in Chicago, Illinois would know about Smuggler's Notch and local tradition of it being used on the Underground Railroad!

§

First thing I wanted to point out is that in Roberson's wonderful poem, he uses the phrase:

> "An underground
> railroad guide's read. tree or face."

That tells me that Roberson had heard of Underground Railroad agents taking fugitives through the Notch, because of using the term "guide." A fugitive would not be a guide, a person familiar with the area would be the guide, taking a person or persons through the Notch to the other side.

§

I came across a Kingfisher reference in *A Year at the Chateau*. Dick Strawbridge writes:

"One time, I was fortunate enough to have been watching a kingfisher cross the moat (they fly like a vivid blue and orange arrow from A to B with great determination and no messing around) when a sparrowhawk swooped to try to take it out of the sky. The kingfisher dived straight into the water and, within seconds, had flown out from the same spot it went in, with equal haste but in exactly the opposite direction. The sparrowhawk had no idea what was going on. Well done, the kingfisher! I was so astounded I wrote about it on Twitter and was delighted to have a response from a gentleman who had been studying kingfishers for the best part of twenty years and had felt privileged to have seen a similar escape trick once himself."

Strawbridge's description of the kingfisher's behavior to dodge and disappear with full intent is representative of how fugitive slaves and Underground Railroad agents operated. Harriet Tubman was known for her ability to dodge and disappear when being pursued.

Contrary to assumptions and assertions of the Underground Railroad network, 90 percent of the work in aiding fugitives was premeditated, strategic and not haphazardly done from what I have learned. Yes, there were fugitives who moved northward on their own, or by directions given, and could show up at someone's door asking for help.

In my research of Vermont and New Hampshire (as well as Massachusetts/Pennsylvania) the network consisted of people who were connected in different ways, and knew who they could entrust with the care of freedom seekers and their next step of the journey. A strategy had to be formed so that on a moment's notice of needed aid, a person would know who to contact, who to go to, etc.

I found that abolitionists and Underground Railroad agents in Massachusetts were connected to New Hampshire and Vermont agents/Abos [short for abolitionists!] so if a party of fugitives or an individual needed help, they knew exactly where they would take them, to whom they would pass them along.

The key of the Underground Railroad success was discretion, trust, dependability, reliability and knowing without a doubt that the people seeking their aid would be safe and moved onward. Every letter from a former UGRR agent to Wilbur Siebert has the same theme, "I don't know much about the network, I only did a small part."

Also, Strawbridge's reference to the kingfisher being determined and direct in its escape, is exactly how UGRR agents had to operate to be of assistance. Of course the fugitives themselves didn't know anyone and were basically in a foreign world once they hit Northern states. So it was the duty of a dedicated agent to get them from Point A to Point B discreetly, efficiently and successfully. After a couple times, this was a pattern and then an established plan/route. Determined and direct also applies to the freedom seekers and their focus on freedom.

This kingfisher reference reminded me of Roberson's lines:

> Glimpse something drop   like fruit from a branch
> of trees along the river   then fall back
> up to its perch –   you've caught the kingfisher

burst from its dive,   back   into position
over the water,   nearly invisible reign;

and

                to fade into or appear
        out of   free

Also, I see how the Kingfisher represents the enslaved
escaping, going from Point A to Point B, being invisible,
under the cover of the night, when en route, blending
into nature so as not to be discovered. "to fade into or
appear, out of, free." And having the determination and
courage to make every move with the ultimate goal of
freedom.

§

Smugglers' Notch, Jeffersonville, VT History

- near Jeffersonville, VT in Lamoille County

- The Notch is near Mt. Mansfield, the highest
  peak in the Green Mountains range in Vermont

- Named for the smuggling prompted by
  President Thomas Jefferson's request to prevent
  American involvement in the Napoleonic Wars.
  U.S. Congress passed the Embargo Act of 1807
  which prohibited American trade with Great
  Britain and Canada. The British bypassed the
  embargo by importing products to Canada
  and they were smuggled down mountain trails

through Smugglers' Notch by Vermonters. This activity slowed at the onset of the War of 1812. [source: Wikipedia]

- The landscape of the Notch has "craggy passages between rocks and small caves offered hidey-holes for slipping past trade embargoes in the 1810s, as part of the Underground Railroad in the 1850s, and to traffic liquor from Canada in the 1930s" during Prohibition. [source: Roadside America.com]

- "Later even before the War Between the States broke out, fugitive slaves began to follow Vermont's Underground Railroad which led through the Notch on an escape route into Canada." [source: suncommunitynews.com]

- "An escaped slave from Troy, NY, Lewis Washington, helped his African brothers and sisters through the Notch and on across Lake Champlain, near Rouses Point, to Canada. Washington had been a slave for 40 years before he bravely worked the Underground Railroad between New York and Vermont." [source: suncommunitynews.com]

- Originally a game trail.

- Due to the Jefferson's Embargo Act, "that trade mostly took the form of cattle sold to British markets and so in the wake of the embargo, farmers who would otherwise bring their herds to the ports of Lake Champlain, instead looked to the mountains and, single file, drove their cattle through the notch and across the unguarded border with Canada...   [T]he role of the trail as a route for smugglers did not disappear. Where once farmers had snuck cattle between the mountains, fugitive slaves smuggled themselves. Smugglers' Notch became a stop along the Underground Railroad, the network of hiding places used by escaped slaves to make their way north across the border. And in the many caves contained within the notch, the escapees would sleep away the daylight hours and prepare to travel by cover of night." [source: news.tubbsnowshoes.com] I know, commercial website but they did their homework and it is well written!

- First road through the Notch built in 1922.

- Ironically, Smugglers' Notch is in the village of Jeffersonville (within the Town of Cambridge) named after President Thomas Jefferson! Vermonters were smuggling against Jefferson's Embargo Act!

§

Underground Railroad Network in Vermont

It is true that various locations in the Northern states during the timeframe of 1820s-1861 were used as hiding places, these locations being natural formations like caves, large crevices, etc. In North Salem, NH is America's Stonehenge which was created pre-1600s by unknown peoples for various celestial, astronomical, religious uses. In the timeframe of the Underground Railroad, a Jonathan Pattee owned that property and used the chambers and caves of stone to hide fugitive slaves.

So Smugglers' Notch caves and hideaways would have been great places to hide.

In my research (of 30 years) those escaping slavery were cared for and taken by the agents on the UGRR network. Once they reached New England States, it was more common to convey someone from your home to the next safehouse. Yes, a person could be given directions to get to the next safehouse but in nine times out of 10, the person(s) would be taken there.

Unlike the initial flight from their owners in the South where they had to get to a certain point where people on the UGRR Network aided them, in New England the common practice was conveyance.

The country and landscape of New England is so different from the Southern states. Most slaves had never been off the property they were born and lived on. They were not allowed to travel even to the neighboring towns alone. So venturing off their "home property" and working their way to places they may have been told about, was like stepping into an unexplored territory not knowing anyone or where you were really going. Not to mention the weather! Anyway, you get the point.

Though a majority of UGRR agents used their home and property to house/hide fugitives, in some cases they did use places like Smugglers' Notch caves etc. Every case was different. Sometimes there were events when the coast was not clear and hiding from bounty hunters, federal marshals, or even, after the Fugitive Slave Law of 1850, citizens who were "deputized" to turn in any free or fugitive person, was necessary.

The other point is that since Smugglers' Notch had an established trail (not a stagecoach road, or heavily traveled thoroughfare) it was perfect for an agent to lead fugitive slaves through to a safehouse northward.

§

Vermont Underground Railroad Agents in Lamoille County and Close Proximity

Now the Wilbur Siebert map that I have attached shows Siebert's research lines running:

- from Hardwick to Morrisville to Hyde Park to Johnson to East Cambridge to Jeffersonville through the Notch to Fairfield and northward to Canada.

- or West to Cambridge, North Underhill, Underhill, to Essex and northward to Canada.

I rely on Siebert's work because it was extensive, a great base to work from and also he was communicating with some of the actual UGRR agents themselves. Definitely check out the Ohio Historical Memory website that has Siebert's entire collection of letters, reports, maps, photographs. Siebert's work has been questioned in the past but I believe if William Still and Harriet Tubman were willing to communicate with Siebert... then I trust his research. Some of his assumptions may be off but the vast collection of actual correspondence is what I use as the starting point.

Siebert's map has Hardwick as a confirmed, documented UGRR stop. I have researched the men who worked there for the Cause – Rev. Kiah Bayley and Dorman Bridgman.

Here are the known agents in the Smugglers' Notch area:

- Johnson, VT: A.W. Caldwell, Jonathan Dodge

- Morrisville, VT: Rev. John Gleed, John West

- Waterville, VT: J.M. Hotchkiss

- Cambridge, VT: Madison Safford

So YES with agents all around the Smugglers' Notch area, I can easily see them using the Notch to take fugitive slaves through to Fairfield, Sheldon, St. Albans, Swanton, up to Canada!

There is more information about these agents but I won't go into that now.

§

Another explanation: In my Vermont book on the UGRR, I was limited in sharing all my research and the fascinating stories of people in Vermont because of the publisher's word count. So a lot of my research didn't make it into the book. AND the research on this subject is constantly growing because more evidence and information surfaces. So I didn't know about Smugglers' Notch back in 2013 (when my book was published) being used in the UGRR network.

I did find in my files the following notes from a 2018 event I did in Orford, NH of what Sharon Rice, who grew up in Stowe, VT, shared with me.

Sharon's great-grandparents told stories of fugitive slaves using the trail through Smuggler's Notch to get to Canada. She was told of their journey through the Notch. She recited what she had been told: "Sneak the slaves by the Kettles, walk on the bridge over the Kettles, hidden up there..." (The water holes in the brook were called "the Kettles.")

She also remembered stories told by her great-grandparents—who owned the Harris homestead in the Stowe area—of fugitive slaves being hidden in the barn. Sharon spoke of a hiding space incorporated into a large hay mound in the barn. The space was large enough to fit people in, where they could sleep, eat and stay until it was time to move on. She recalls that the fugitives would be transported by a wagon that had a double bottom (loading the people in the bottom layer and the top layer covered with hay) to the next safehouse.

I haven't confirmed the UGRR safehouse mentioned or the Kettles but oral history is important to save.

What a wonderful thing to have a subject that is constantly evolving and new people and events to research! I didn't know of Lewis Washington (references above) until I was looking into things for you!!

§§§

Roots and Sources

I transcribed pertinent moments from *Ed Roberson and Lyn Hejinian in Conversation*, the October 2020 audio recording available on the website of The Poetry Foundation. On the sunny cold afternoon of Saturday February 24, 2024, while working on last corrections, I received news of Lyn Hejinian's death at the age of 82. Please remember that my little book that you are now reading is unimaginable without her coming before me, and not only because it quotes her extensively. Consider this a second dedication. I quoted a passage from page 94 of Stanley Cavell's 1995 *Philosophical Passages: Wittgenstein, Emerson, Austin, Derrida.* Just before that, I borrowed Cavell's words "being accosted" from a passage in the same book on pages 128 and 129. In that passage, Cavell considers Ludwig Wittgenstein's encounter with Saint Augustine's description of a childhood memory in *Confessions.* Cavell writes, "It begins with some words of someone else. But why say this? Perhaps to suggest that Wittgenstein [...] is not led to philosophical reflection from his own voice (or what might be recognized, right off, as his own voice), but from, as it were, being *accosted*. The accosting is by someone Wittgenstein cares about and has taken seriously; in particular, it is by such a one speaking about his childhood, so in words of memory, and more particularly, about his first memory of words, say of first acquiring them. [...] Put otherwise: To open this book philosophically is to feel that a mind has paused here—which no doubt already suggests a certain kind of mind, or a mind in certain straits." The Thoreau extracts regarding his famous loon stalking derive from the latter pages of the *Brute Neighbors* chapter of *Walden.* You will find the sentences about dawn in the book's concluding chapter. The poet Dan Beachy-Quick reviewed for *The Colorado Review* Ed Roberson's *MPH and Other Road Poems*, published by Verge Books in 2021. Dan wrote, "In the poem time can surrender its mortal march to wilder horizons, east and west as one, youth and age, life and death, the same. A lifetime ago Ed Roberson rode on a motorcycle cross country. In *MPH* we understand, as he does, he's riding still." Bruce H. Kirmmse translated *Fear and Trembling* for a volume published in 2022 on which I have relied for the passages on the spirituality of inwardness, passages that gave way to Robert Creeley's comments quoted by Don Byrd requoted by The Poetry Foundation. I extracted the phrase "a voice already on its way to becoming another voice" from the foreword that Andrew Welsh wrote for *Voices Cast Out to Talk Us In*, Ed Roberson's 1995 book published by the University of Iowa Press. Welsh's phrase "lattice of voices," perfectly descriptive of Roberson's poetry, became aspirational for me in composing this essay. Anne Dufourmantelle wrote of the prisoner in Plato's myth of the Cave, his turning toward light, on page 2 of *In Praise of Risk*. I quote the line from the English translation by Steven Miller, published by Fordham University Press in 2019, posthumously after Dufourmantelle drowned in 2017 after rescuing two children from a suddenly rough surf in the sea near St. Tropez. I quote one sentence from page 119 of *How to Disappear* by Akiko Busch published by Penguin Press in 2019. The sonnet identified by its first line *Bright star, would I were stedfast as thou art—*, the final version of which John Keats, its author, transcribed onto a page of *The Poetical Works of William Shakespeare* in late September 1820 while aboard the Rome-bound ship *Maria Crowther*, contains the lines

The moving waters at their priestlike task
    Of pure ablution round earth's human shores,

In his essay *Ed Roberson 101* for The Poetry Foundation
website, originally published August 2nd, 2016,
Benjamin Voight writes, "Quick-changing syntax,
hyper-extended metaphors, and sudden inversions
of argument—much of what makes Roberson's work
innovative can also make it challenging." Ralph Ellison's
1952 novel Invisible Man opens with the keynote line
regarding subjectivity and visibility. In an interview by
Charles H. Rowell titled "The Unravelling of the Egg"
first published in Callaloo 19, Autumn 1983, Jay Wright
asked the question, to which I find myself endlessly
returning, "Who is the we I mean?"

My friend Jack Murchie, an architect, texted me on
Friday, August 27th, 2021, at 7:48 PM CST in response to
my question about kingfisher sightings. My conversation
with Iris Moore I wrote from memory. The lines regarding
"augury's loon" come from the poem *The Counsel of
Birds* in *City Eclogue*, Ed Roberson's 2006 book, number
23 in the Atelos series. Charles Hartshorne's description
of the Kingfisher group's lack of song appears on page
212 of *Born to Sing*, first published in 1973 by Indiana
University Press. Hartshorne studied ornithology at the
University of Michigan Biological Station. On page 150
of her book noted below, Wahida Khandker quotes his
process-theological definition of creativity as that which
"determines what is undetermined, and thus *adds to
the definiteness* of reality." Walt Whitman's *Learn'd
Astronomer* makes his appearance in *Leaves of Grass*.
Roberson's lines describing tasks undertaken "from that

cabin by the lake on the job / at the research station"
begin the poem *"There Are Many Stops Along the Way"*
from *The New Wing of the Labyrinth* published in 2009
by Singing Horse Press. Stephen Young introduced me
to Ed Roberson at The Poetry Foundation on February
20th, 2016, and as noted, Alex Benjamin facilitated
our correspondence in October 2020. Ben Lytal,
video conferencing from a closet, reminded me of the
passage in Renee Gladman's *Calamities*, published
by Wave Books, that describes the Roberson lesson.
Renee Gladman presented a lecture titled *Cities of the
Future* at The School of the Art Institute of Chicago
on Thursday, March 28th, 2019. I borrow the term
conatus from Spinoza, who wrote of it in Proposition
VII of Part III of his *Ethics* (translated by George Eliot):
"The effort by which everything strives to persevere
in existing, is nothing but the actual essence of that
thing." Wahida Khandker wrote of the act of drawing
and diagram-making on page 85 of *Process Metaphysics
and Mutative Life—Sketches of Lived Time*, published in
2020 by Palgrave Macmillan. History Press published,
and Arcadia distributes, Michelle Arnosky Sherburne's
2013 book *Abolition & the Underground Railroad in
Vermont*. Late in the quoted part of their conversation,
Lyn Hejinian makes reference to Ed Roberson's poem
Choke. That poem offers the following three couplets as
conclusion.

a sense of time can be that distance's familiar
but the mind can empathize itself that size the dreadlocks

of black holes   where the anger digests itself
the joy carries its brother sadness also over

and fear realizes it's ok
and the rains come   the forests   the jungles   the birds!

§§§

Matthew Goulish co-founded *Every house has a door* in 2008 with Lin Hixson. He is dramaturg, writer, and sometimes performer with the company. He was a founding member of *Goat Island*, the Chicago-based performance group that existed from 1987 to 2009. His books include *39 microlectures – in proximity of performance* (Routledge, 2001), *The Brightest Thing in the World – 3 Lectures from the Institute of Failure* (Green Lantern Press, 2012), *Work from Memory: In Response to In Search of Lost Time by Marcel Proust*, co-authored with Dan Beachy-Quick (Ahsahta Press, 2012) and *Pitch and Revelation—Reconfigurations of Reading, Poetry, and Philosophy through the Work of Jay Wright*, co-authored with Will Daddario (Punctum Books, 2022). His essays have appeared in *Richard Rezac Address* (University of Chicago Press, 2018), *Propositions in the Making – Experiments in a Whiteheadian Laboratory* (Rowman & Littlefield, 2020), and many other journals and anthologies. He teaches in the Writing Program of The School of the Art Institute of Chicago.

'kingfisher' from *asked what has changed* (Wesleyan University Press, 2021) published with the generous permission of Ed Roberson.
Renee Gladman's *Calamities* published with the generous permission of the author and Wave Books.
Michelle Sherburne published with the generous permission of the author.

Inner book template, cover design template, and logo by Robbie Dawson.

978-1-915000-00-2

both are worse

Brighton
2024

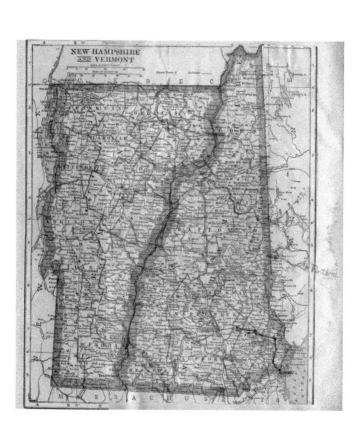

NEW HAMPSHIRE
AND VERMONT

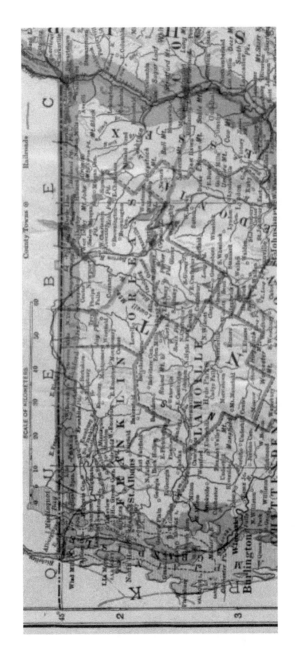